BY

HIS

STRIPES!

A HEALER'S ANOINTING
OF SUCCESS STRATEGIES

LINDA D. LEE, PCLC, CCM

Multi award-winning author

LL Media Group LLC
Where Freedom Reigns

ISBN: 978-0-9979068-5-1

But He was woun-dea for our transgressions,
He was bruised for our iniquities;
The chastisement for our peace was upon Him,
And __by His stripes__ we are healed. (Isaiah 53:5).

Table of Content

LINDA D. LEE

Introduction

The proven success strategies in *By His Stripes: A Healer's Anointing of Success Strategies* will give you a blueprint to ensure a solid transformation in your spiritual life. The erratic world that we live in doesn't have a blueprint and doesn't play well with our ever-changing lives. Peace of mind seems impossible to achieve. The good news is that this healer's anointing will offer the reader real testimonies, situations and challenges that allows you to witness the transformation that will elevate your faith walk. Overcomers do not have the luxury of negating the experience of what they overcome.

These success strategies will help you to gain clarity and understanding by offering you a blueprint to get to your destination. Two strategies being mentioned today are "sing the Word" and healthy vegan options. I first learned about "singing the Word" from Julie Meyer, a guest on Sid Roth's It's Supernatural Show. Meanwhile, you might be wondering how healthy eating is a new strategy. Well, it must be new if you have not figured out it actually works. It is not a myth! The Center for Science in the Public Interest previously quoted, "Unhealthy diet contributes to approximately 678, 000 deaths each year in the U.S., due to nutrition- and obesity-related diseases, such as heart disease, cancer, and type 2 diabetes."[1] And today, the situation has not changed. You need to be healthy to operate your business and tend to your family. The overcomer's in this book are living examples of what happens when you experience a healer's anointing and make some lifestyle changes. Without these lifestyle changes their businesses would have continued to suffer. Now open your mind and understand miraculous healing to activate a healer anointing in your life, business or career.

CHAPTER 2

The Blood Still Works!
By Linda D. Lee

Thanksgiving and Christmas are supposed to be a time of celebration and worship to Jehovah God. Unfortunately, for me they became a time of heartache, hurt and unforgiveness. I grew to dislike these days in particular. Both were tied to traumatic experiences, which I will briefly share to help someone else. Imagine it is Thursday, December 19, 1991. A chain of events took place leading up to our daughter being still born.

Oh, my Lord, I was in so much pain I could barely stand up straight. The pain was excruciating, but I kept pressing forward in my wifely duties. I knew I had to go to work, take care of home and tend to our son. There was one problem. My last **OBGYN** visit revealed amniotic fluid had been leaking from around our baby for about a month. The news alone terrified me! I did not leave the doctor's office until he answered my questions: "How could our baby be safe with all the fluid I was leaking? How long could our baby survive with this problem? Did my job contribute to this problem? Did standing on those concreate floors damage my body?" Questions, questions and more questions. Of all days, I really needed my ex-husband to attend this doctor's appointment. Unfortunately, he had to work. There was so many thoughts running through my mind. It was definitely too early in the pregnancy for me to have complications. No, I was not a high-risk pregnancy! So, what happened? All I could do was cry as I took my time driving back to work.

The rest of the day I could not stop thinking about the doctor's report. Anxiety was building as I tried not to fall apart and keep a brave face in front of my colleagues. However, some knew something was terribly wrong.

As I regained by composure, I returned to the composing room floor. I was a Paste-up Artist working for a subsidiary newspaper company. Most people don't know that back in the day newspaper pages were manually built on composition tables while standing on concrete floors. Thank God, they finally got rubber mats to stand on! But was it too late? This was my routine for many, many years adding trauma to my body and feet. One might wonder why I would accept a job that would be traumatic to my body. And, I would ask them, "What do you do when your family needs to eat and you're the primary breadwinner?" Yes, my ex-husband worked, but he did not make a lot of money. My job was the best option we had to keep making ends meet. Therefore, in being sensitive to the needs of our home, I endured the pain and discomfort temporarily. Unfortunately, on the day of my doctor's appointment the pain left me speechless, even after returning to work.

The more I stood on my feet to work the more fluid released. Have you ever tried to "not walk" and just work in one spot? I have. It is not a good feeling and did not work for me at all. Preventive measures kicked in as I ran back-and-forth to the restroom to avert an accident. Then it happened! A huge ball of pressure from my abdomen released an indescribable amount of fluid. I could feel fluid running down my legs. It felt like my water broke! I was in the second trimester of pregnancy. It was way, way too early for me to give birth! I was terrified and started screaming for help. Since I was the only female in our department, some men ran to assist me while others ran to get a female editor. I can't remember who called my ex-husband, but eventually I spoke with him briefly before calling my doctor.

My doctor kept trying to convince me our baby was fine. But, I couldn't phantom what he was saying; it went in one ear and out the other. SOMETHING felt terribly wrong and I needed to be seen by my doctor. Although I worked over an hour away, he finally agreed to see me as a walk-in. After calling my husband back with the update, he rushed to pick me; we shared one car. I have never seen him drive SO FAST. I prayed all the way there. We padded the passenger seat with some old clothes and anything we found in the car; fluid was still leaking. The pain had intensified so I was hunched over in the front seat.

We finally made it to the doctor's office only to hear him say after the examination, "Nothing is wrong." Anger rose up in me as I responded, "WHAT? Nothing is wrong? What do you mean nothing is wrong?" What in the world was he talking about? My pain was real. The leaking fluid running down my legs was real. What happened was real. My ex-husband surely didn't know what to say as everyone tried to calm me down. I felt my heart pounding as we dealt with all this uncertainty.

My doctor convinced us the baby was safe. He also explained it wasn't unusual for pregnant women to leak amniotic fluid. This was definitely news to me! Although we felt uneasy, we left and went home.

As the day progressed into the night my stomach started hurting. At first, I played it off due to the earlier events at the doctor's office. But the pain did go away as insomnia set in in the wee-hours of the morning. I know it was nobody but the Lord that brought to my remembrance the child-birth book I was reading. Plain as day, the Spirit took me to the section on false labor verses real labor. Now someone is thinking, "I thought she already had a son; she should know false labor from real labor pains." And you are correct. However, when you look at the totality of my situation, being in labor was the LAST thing I would imagine.

In the book it said, "Start timing the pain to determine if its real or false." Ok, I did that. Real labor pains continue while false pains stop. My pain was coming five minutes apart! I thought, "This is crazy; I can't be in labor. It's too early! I woke my ex-husband up and shared what was going on. And like most people, he said nothing is wrong, try to go back to sleep. How could I sleep with all this going on? As such, I continued to time the intervals of the pain, which increased to 2-3 minutes. Now I know for sure **SOMETHING IS WRONG!** After waking my ex-husband, I called my doctor's office. I already knew the answering service would be able to reach him before office hours. He immediately called me back, but there was no urgency in his voice.

Since we were under a Health Maintenance Organization (HMO) plan I needed my doctor's "permission" to go to the emergency room for care. Not only did he not approve any visit to the emergency room but he insisted I wasn't in labor and needed some rest. Now I'm really thinking I'm crazy!

Nobody thinks anything is wrong.

Everyone keeps telling me to get some rest.

The pain is real. Why won't they listen to me?

Meanwhile, I laid in bed crying. Help me Lord! The pain was insurmountable and I couldn't take it anymore. I jumped up, woke my ex-husband, and informed him I was driving myself to the emergency room. Of course, he wouldn't allow me to do that. But the moments afterwards became a big blur until we arrived at the hospital. By the time we walked into the emergency room the pain subsided. I remember telling the receptionist, "I think I'm in labor. The pains are 2-3 minutes apart." Since I wasn't in distress, she asked how far along I was. Immediately I stated, "second trimester" hoping a doctor would see me right away. Instead, I was asked to take a seat and a doctor would see me soon. As I was leaving the receptionist desk the pain hit me again and paralyzed me against the wall. Only then, did the receptionist hurry to find the doctor.

I kept watching the clock...tick...tock...tick...tock.

Still no doctor.

Tick...tock...tick...tock.

Still no doctor.

Finally, my ex-husband insisted I be seen immediately.

The receptionist agreed and put us in an examination room. Our baby was really kicking and moving around a lot. As I sat on the examination table time kept passing, then it happened!

Blood GUSHED out of me and started running onto the floor. All I could do was cry. My ex-husband started screaming for help and went to find the receptionist or doctor. Our son was there but he was too young to understand what was going on. Finally, the doctor came with the receptionist not far behind. Were their actions too late? Yes!

Someone called for a gurney, another person called my OBGYN doctor, while others quickly whisked me into the delivery room. Unfortunately, another problem was identified upon our arrival. All the while, I could feel our baby moving around extremely hard. I truly believe our baby was fighting for its life.

In our disbelief the delivery room had NOT been cleaned or sanitized from the previous procedure. I know you're thinking the same thing I did: "WHAT? THE DELIVERY ROOM IS NOT SANITIZED? Who does that? Who leaves a labor and delivery room dirty and not sanitized?" No one had an answer. This night had turned into a NIGHTMARE. Meanwhile, we all knew the baby was probably in distress because its movement had slowed tremendously. I started asking where my OBGYN doctor was. It didn't seem right wasn't there tending to our baby.

But, due to the quick thinking of the emergency room doctor, they wheeled me into a side room about the size and width of a small pantry. It became our "labor and delivery room." It was so tight only one person could stand on each side of the bed. Two nurses quickly moved beside the gurney and hooked me up to the blood pressure machine and other equipment. The doctor moved into position to deliver our baby early. Everything happened so fast! The door was open so my ex-husband could see what was going on since no other people could fit in the room.

Unfortunately, it was too late!

The doctor delivered our baby girl, who we later named Atoyaa Janaa. She was still born with the umbilical cord wrapped around her neck. I was too distraught to hold her. Shortly after, she was placed in a bowl beside the bed like discarded waste. I can still see *your* eyes staring at me and *your* long legs dangling from the rim of the bowl. I was temporarily mesmerized because I always wanted a daughter. Then, I heard a familiar voice and looked toward the door. Guess who it was? It was my OBGYN doctor FINALLY showing up after being informed of recent events. Come to find out, I had been in LABOR all day and "no one" listened. Although my doctor was apologetic for not believing me, I LET HIM HAVE IT: "Why didn't you listen to me? I told you something was wrong. All you had to do was approve me for an emergency visit. You "killed" my baby." Of course, he didn't want to hear that. I couldn't stand to see his face and told him to leave! This was around Christmas and I was slowly sinking into depression. I was mad at God and everybody else that didn't hear my cry for help.

And, I believe this traumatic incident was the catalyst for our next traumatic event. Going against my grannies suggestion, we immediately tried to have another baby. I didn't want to grieve; I wanted a daughter. Unfortunately, we were met with more misfortune. Our son Raymon Jr. was born prematurely around Thanksgiving of the next year. He survived in the Neonatal Intensive Care Unit (N.I.C.U) almost three months and never came home! Although I remember the events so clearly, I simply wish to share that he passed away from Sudden Infant Death Syndrome (S.I.D.S) on my first day back at work. I tried to move on so I could be there for our son Martell, but I was a mess!

How many of you know that time heals old wounds? Well, it does. I'm a witness. Only. God could heal my heart and restore my faith in mankind over time. But that's not the end of the story!

Many, many years later all of my traumatic experiences came back to haunt me when my menstrual cycle became irregular. I was the "Woman with an ISSUE of Blood" as mentioned in Mark 5:25-32. My cycle would flow like running water for weeks or a month. This issue was so bad, I would drive 40 miles after leaving home and would have to almost change clothes due to the overflow of blood. I started padding my car seat just to be on the safe side. Does this sound familiar to you from an earlier part of my testimony? I quoted, "By his stripes I am healed" many times. But the blood kept flowing. This went on "for years" until I had become anemic and fatigued. My new OBGYN doctor presented me with very few options. Not one time did she mention Jesus, but I did! I had enough Jesus in me to call on his name. So, I agreed to undergo surgery knowing I was already healed. At that time, I wasn't spiritually mature enough to know about manifestation. All I knew was, "By his stripes I was healed. By his stirpes I was healed." I couldn't even tell you where to find it in the Bible; I just knew in my heart I believed the word of God!

My recovery time wasn't necessarily for me; it was to help others' unbelief. They just wanted confirmation that **THE BLOOD STILL WORKS**. They needed to hear my testimony of no longer being the "Woman with an issue with blood!" They needed to know God dried up my brook supernaturally by faith! His divine power was truly at work in my life. As months turned into years, I couldn't even remember having "the issue." Talk about miraculous healing. So, be encouraged in knowing **BY HIS STIRPES** you are healed! Walk your healing out and eat right. Self-care is important, self-awareness is critical, and spending time with Father God is key to increasing your faith by reading and speaking the word of God. Now, by faith, brace yourself for three more phenomenal overcomer stories that will change your life!

CHAPTER 3

The Blood Still Works Exercise

On my journey I chose to move on instead of fully grieving the death of our daughter. Although God's divine power allowed me to walk through that season, an interview from South Korea made me aware that I still had residue of hurt and unforgiveness lingering inside me.

Be still and look back over your life for traumatic experiences where you did not grieve and simply moved on? Annotate the experience here.

_____

_____

_____

_____

_____

_____

_____

_____

_____

_____

_____

_____

_____

_____

_____

_____

_____

Now that you **identified** problem areas, give yourself permission to grieve, heal, and forgive anyone involved. Moving on without grieving has proven to be unhealthy. Adapt to a new lifestyle to improve your health.

CHAPTER 4

From Illness to Optimal Health

By Stephanie M. Pelle

I was physically fit, or at least I thought I was. Unfortunately, I made some unhealthy food decisions while I was working in a high paced work environment. You see, I worked in the emergency room as an admissions representative. Nights and weekends while trying to earn a degree in business, and it almost cost me my life. Unknown to me, I had hypertension also known as "The Silent Killer." It's pretty apparent why it is called that—and for good reason. Sometimes people don't have any symptoms. Increased blood pressure can lead to many health problems; for me it was kidney disease. I was put on Emergency Kidney Dialysis, which automatically requires transplant if you are to successfully live a quality life. I was on kidney dialysis almost six years. I was informed at five years, that not only did I need a kidney transplant, but a liver transplant as well. Unfortunately, I wasn't a candidate for a liver biopsy because the pain would be too unbearable. The odds of multiple transplants were against me!

I cried out to the Lord in prayer. I asked for "dos regalos," which in Spanish means two gifts—or a liver and a kidney. God had answered Job's prayer for a blessing, and I had faith that He would grant me the same double portion blessing. I was frail and in a great deal of pain. I felt as though there was a dark cloud hovering over me. I lay in bed unable to move and wailing in pain. I called out to the Lord to either take me home with Him or relieve me of this burden. Then, the phone rang—a nurse calling from United Organ Sharing, and she said she had an organ donor for me—"A One in a Million Match"—then went on to say that I needed to get to the hospital as soon as possible to be prepared for surgery.

After I got to the hospital, the preparation began quickly. I was escorted pre-op, where nurses took blood, and I was typed and screened to receive blood if necessary during the surgery. The transplant physician came in to talk with me briefly, then a chaplain came in to pray with me. I was suited up in what looked like a bear suit, to keep me warm as the operating room would be very cold. The surgery was 13 hours, and I was placed under anesthesia for 23 hours. The recovery from the surgery was hard; I felt as though I'd been hit by a truck. I had to endure physical and occupational therapies, and I was 98 lbs. and frail. Initially, I had to use a wheelchair, then I graduated to a walker, then a cane. Ten months later, I was walking three miles daily, and dancing in a Zumba class. My health sprung back and I was feeling youthful again.

I knew that I couldn't go back to my old lifestyle of making poor food choices and not incorporating exercise into my lifestyle. Thus, I sought out a nutritionist and worked with a chiropractor for alignments.

Now, I encourage and inspire others to take back their health and to avoid what I went through by adopting a plant-based whole-food diet. It may not be for those who are sick and tired of being sick. I've had to do some hard work over the years to regain my health. It hasn't been easy by any means. Sometimes we walk through things in life that are beyond our intellect to handle.

Creating a critiquing Caribbean recipe has brought me a lot of passion for cooking healthy meals and sharing them with others. Sharing truly is caring because I couldn't possibly take credit for all the recipes that others have shared with me.

At the time of this book release, I'll be celebrating six years post-transplant and doing well. Many of my family and friends that walked through this process with me have mentioned how strong I was through the process. Honestly, I knew I was not alone. It is only my faith in God that brought me through. Furthermore, I'm so grateful to the donor family for their gift of love.

I hope you are inspired to keep hope alive in the event you are faced with a health crisis. The scripture that helped me through this process is Isaiah 26:3: "You will keep him in perfect peace, whose mind is stayed on You, because he trusts in You," (MEV).

I was healed of my infirmity by the stripes Yeshua bore on Calvary, and by His amazing Grace I was delivered and set free of my infirmity. Furthermore, my financial burden was lifted (the expenses I incurred were enormous, and I had out of pocket costs that insurance medical insurance didn't cover). I had to hire private help to take me to appointments and or clean my home, because, while I was recovering, I could not manage on my own. Although I had the support of friends who got groceries from the store for me. I didn't have much family support, so I had no choice but to hire help. Over a period of time I incurred over $10,000 in medical debt, and no taxable income. I was making payments of $40-50 month. But then I received a letter stating your bill of $11,943.05 has been adjusted to $0.00. All glory to God for who He is, and what he has done for me.

Recommendations:

- Get yearly wellness checks on your birthday, which is an easy day to remember.
- Eat a nutritionally balanced diet consisting of essential vitamins, minerals, and plenty of water.
- Try to get at least eight hours' sleep each night.
- Exercise regularly. Walk 20-30 minutes daily. Take an exercise class of your choice: Zumba, Pilates,

Studio Barre. I don't recommend Yoga because of its roots in other Gods—I speak from personal experience. Hosea 4:6 says, "My people are destroyed for lack of knowledge: because thou hast rejected knowledge, I will also reject thee, that thou shalt be no priest to me: seeing thou hast forgotten the law of thy God, I will also forget thy children."

- Pamper yourself, treat yourself to a spa day once a month of every other month by getting a manicure, pedicure or massage. There are affordable options in places like Groupon. I realize this sounds very easy, but you have a plan in place if you are going to achieve these recommendations on a regular basis.

CHAPTER 5

Optimal Health Exercise

Let's activate a healer anointing in your life, business or career! According to WebMD online, "If your blood pressure is extremely high, there may be certain symptoms to look out for when it comes to hypertension: Severe headache, fatigue or confusion, vision problems, chest pain, difficulty breathing, irregular heartbeat, blood in the urine, and pounding in your chest, neck, or ears. In fact, nearly one-third of people who have high blood pressure don't know it." Stop! Access your health situation. List below any symptoms you are having or have had recently:

_____

_____

_____

_____

_____

_____

_____

_____

_____

_____

_____

_____

_____

_____

_____

_____

_____

_____

_____

_____

_____

_____

Now that you have **identified** problem areas, make a doctor's appointment immediately!

Lifestyle Preventive Measures

Lose extra pounds and watch your waistline

Exercise regularly

Walk

Jog

Cycle

Swim

Dance

High-intensity interval training

Eat a healthy diet

Keep a food diary

Consider healthy food option

Consider boosting your potassium level

Be a smart shopper and read labels

Reduce sodium (salt) in your diet

Read food labels

Eat fewer processed foods

Don't add salt; ease into it over time

Limit the amount of alcohol you drink

Quit smoking

Cut back on caffeine

Reduce your stress

Monitor your blood pressure at home and see a doctor

regularly

Get support

Extracurricular activity

Journal

Vlog

Blog

Art and crafts

Write a book

Sing

Run

Gardener

Workout

Drink more water

Christian meditation

Brain teaser games

CHAPTER 6

A Caregiver Who Watched God Heal
By Vandra Noel

Caregivers are unsung heroes that work hard behind the scene to ensure the ones they are giving care to is first priority. I truly believe caregivers are handpicked by God because it's an assignment that is not for just anyone. I have worn many hats as a caregiver caring for family members who have battled alcoholism, drugs, asthma, depression, congestive heart failure, 4th stage lymphoma cancer, lung cancer, kidney cancer, mastitis, rheumatoid Arthritis, sickle cell anemia, breast cancer, and Alzheimer's. Without the help of God and the profession of doctors and nurses and a few good friends, I would not have survived.

See, caregivers give more of themselves to those they care for and end up losing themselves. Depression, anxiety and insomnia are the three major things I have battled.

Every loved one that has needed me needed to know that I was there for them no matter what, because fear of the unknown kept them in bondage.

As I journeyed with my loved ones who battled alcoholism and drug addiction, I realized I was trying to protect them from the ridicule of outsiders who laughed and mocked them. Not knowing shame and depression are the root to most addictions, I loved them where they were while I set up mental boundaries for myself. People with addictions don't need to be reminded about their issues; they need to be reminded how great they are.

Caring for my family who battled cancer was extremely different! Watching my loved one deteriorating before my eyes made me scared, angry and depressed. There was nothing I could do to take away their pain, sickness or fears. The chemotherapy was harsh to the point it sapped all their energy and made them sicker than before they went in for the treatments. From hair loss to weight loss to the verge of death kept me before God on their behalf. I cried myself to sleep many nights praying that the next day would be better than the day before. I was angry with God for all the sickness that my loved ones had, and because I was the one who had to be there while others lived their lives.

Anger is real in caregivers, and without a prayer life anger will fester and cause you to be an unpleasant person to be around. As a matter a fact, I didn't want to be in my own presence because I was so mean! Once I understood that this assignment was tailor made for me, I started appreciating the assignment because I got information first hand and I was able to make sure they were taken care of for real and with love.

Caring for someone with Alzheimer's is a challenge! The first onset of the illness was called Sundown syndrome where the chemical balance in the brain becomes off and makes them a totally different person. However, soon as the morning came they are okay. It is amazing how different illnesses cause people to act differently. My loved one was not violent but knew she was sick when she saw the clothes she had on when she woke up. She would have on a trench coat, rain boots and a scarf because in her mind she was walking to work in the cold and rain but in actuality it was a cool spring nights. The Sundown turned into Alzheimer's, which caused her to not know her loved ones. I had to put her in a nursing home with a secured unit because I could not watch her and my small children. I felt like I was throwing her away when I moved her to the facility, but I had no other choice. There are studies that show many caregivers die before the one they are caring for because of the failure to care for themselves. As my loved one deteriorated, I felt empty and alone because the role she played in my life was coming to an end. When she passed away, I had to find my new Normal because all I knew was caring for her, checking on her and loving on her. I didn't know what to do with my idle time until another loved one needed me.

Mastitis was something I knew nothing about. When my loved one was diagnosed, I saw her flesh being eaten away by the infection that was caused from clogged milk ducts and a staph infection. The pain and the chills were so evident from the cries, and the shivering was nonstop. I was so scared because I thought they would have to remove her breast to stop the infection from worsening.

Our bodies can heal themselves if we take the proper precautions and instructions from those experienced in their field of practice. Changing gauze and keeping the infected area clean as well as taking antibiotics was key! Without that the infection was subject to traveling to her bloodstream. I read up on stories of others who had this infection to get the knowledge I needed to understand the why's and how's of this happening. Today you can't even tell where the infection was—and that's all God!

As a caregiver you learn so much and the wealth of knowledge you gain is to share and help others who may have the same issues. Support groups are needed, and whether those groups are formed by people in your life or through an agency, you need support.

Sickle cell anemia is a disease many people don't know about. The sickling of the blood cells during a crisis restricts oxygen from getting to the organs. The pain in the bones and the blood transfusions needed to help warriors survive would blow your mind. Sickle cell patients are labeled as people hooked on pain meds and are looks upon as junkies. It is heartbreaking to hear a doctor or a nurse say the pain isn't that bad and then just give Tylenol or Advil with a high milligram instead of administering the morphine and codeines. I have watched my loved one scream, cry and shake because of the excruciating pain they felt. If I could take the pain away I would, but prayer is all I have as well as support and my presence.

When dealing with a loved one with congestive heart failure and fourth stage kidney failure, you have to stay strong. The swelling of the body, limited air to breath and the pain incorporated in it all is so hard to witness. Oxygen and meds to pull for fluid off the body are just a part of the treatment. Vitals and bloodwork have to be done often to watch the kidney function and heart strength.

Hospital stays in the big chair or hard pull out bed are normal for a caregiver. They are extremely uncomfortable but rendering the support and the care for those overrides it all.

Caregivers are real selfless people who put their lives on hold to help those who are sick to live!

I made it through it all and I know if it had not been for the Lord on my side, I would not be sharing my caregiving stories with you. While I watched all my loved ones be overcomer's, I became an overcomer, too!

Please pray for a caregiver and their families because giving up is a thought, but overcoming is a determination.

LINDA D. LEE

CHAPTER 7

Watch God Heal Exercise

In Vandra's story, she was the caregiver for family members who have battled alcoholism, drugs, asthma, depression, congestive heart failure, 4th stage lymphoma cancer, lung cancer, kidney cancer, mastitis, rheumatoid Arthritis, sickle cell anemia, breast cancer, and Alzheimer's. One thing they all had in common was a desire for a healthy eating regimen. List all your bad eating or emotional eating habits:

_____

_____

_____

_____

_____

_____

_____

_____

_____

_____

_____

_____

_____

_____

_____

_____

_____

_____

_____

Go to your kitchen and THROW-AWAY any food or drinks that **triggers** your unhealthy lifestyle. It's time for a new food option. Have you ever considered whole food, plant-based or vegan?

36

CHAPTER 8

Thrive on Healthy Vegan Recipes

By Chef Nneka
(Abuja, Nigeria)

SWEET & SOUR TOFU
Serves 3 people

INGREDIENTS:
TOFU
- 300g tofu (cut in cube)
- 1 tablespoon apple cider vinegar (or lemon juice)
- 3 tablespoon soy sauce
- 2 cloves garlic
- 4 tablespoon cornstarch
- 2 tablespoon olive oil (or coconut oil)
- 1 medium carrot, chopped
- 1 red bell pepper, chopped
- 1 green bell pepper, chopped
- 1 medium onion, chopped
- Salt and pepper
- Seasoning powder
- 2 spring onions, chopped

SWEET AND SOUR SAUCE
- 3 tablespoon date syrup
- 2 tablespoon tomato paste
- 2 teaspoon soy sauce
- 1 tablespoon apple cider vinegar or lemon juice
- 1/3 cup water
- 1 tablespoon cornstarch

DIRECTIONS
TOFU
1. Mix vinegar, garlic and soy sauce in a bowl, then add Cubed tofu. Stir, making sure the vinegar mixture coats the tofu. Set it aside for at least 5 minutes.
2. Add cornstarch to the tofu and toss to coat the tofu (make sure it is coated with cornstarch; add a little more if needed).
3. Heat olive oil in a pan over medium heat and cook the tofu (stir to avoid burning). Cook until it's golden brown, then remove it from heat and set it aside.
4. Cook vegetables (bell peppers, onions and carrot) in the same pan used for the tofu. Cook until they are tender.
Then add in the tofu, salt, pepper and seasoning powder to the pan and set aside.

SWEET & SOUR SAUCE
1. Mix all ingredients until they are properly mixed.
2. Add sweet and sour sauce to the vegetable and tofu (in the pan). Cook over low heat for 5 minutes, stirring to avoid burning. Pour in spring onions, stir and bring it down.
Serve warm with burgur wheat basmati rice or grain of choice.

BEANS STIR FRY
Serves 2 people

INGREDIENTS
- 1 tablespoon tomato paste
- 1 tablespoon soy sauce
- 2 teaspoons sesame seed oil
- Salt and pepper
- 1 clove garlic, crushed
- 1 tablespoon sesame seed (optional)
- 100g tofu, cubed (or 100g mushroom) (optional)
- 1 tablespoon olive oil
- 1 medium red onions, diced
- 1/2 cup carrot, diced
- 1 fresh tomato, diced
- 1 spring onions
- Seasoning powder (or stock cube)
- 2 cups cooked beans (any type of beans)

DIRECTION
1. Mix together the tomato paste, sesame oil, soy sauce, pepper, salt and garlic (Marinade sauce).
2. Add cubes of tofu or mushroom and soak them in the marinade sauce. Add the sesame seeds and stir briefly. Let it sit or about 30 minutes to 1 hour.
3. In a pan over medium heat, heat oil, add carrots, red onions and fresh tomatoes. Fry for at least 5 minutes.

4. Add Tofu and sauce, beans and seasoning powder and cook for more 10 minutes.

Finish up by adding spring onions.

5. Serve warm with a slice of whole wheat bread.

BEANS & POTATO CHILLI (Nigerian style)

Serves 2 people (you can use any type of potato you want, yam or plantain)

INGREDIENTS:
- 3 large potato (peeled and chopped in cubes)
- 1 medium onion (diced)
- 2 clove garlic (crushed)
- 1 teaspoon ginger (crushed)
- 3 fresh tomato (diced)
- 2 cups cooked beans (130g)
- 1.5 to 2 cups water or vegetable stock
- 1 tablespoon olive or coconut oil
- Salt
- Seasoning cube
- Pepper (black or hot pepper as desired)

DIRECTION
1. Heat oil in a pan over low to medium heat.
2. Add potato and onion and cook while stirring (for about 4 minutes) until the onion softens.
3. Add ginger, garlic and salt. Cook, stirring often, for 30 seconds.
4. Add water (or stock) and bring to a simmer for about 10 minutes or until the potato is tender.

5. Add beans, tomatoes and stock cube; increase heat to medium and allow to simmer, stirring often.
6. Allow to simmer for 5 minutes.
7. Remove from heat and stir in chopped parsley.
8. Serve warm.

CHAPTER 9

Speak Life to Your Situation
By Latonya Thomas

On August 11, 2017, my life changed forever. Standing inside Nordstrom Rack I received news that my bloodwork came back and I had been diagnosed with (SLE) Systematic Lupus Erythematosus. This is an autoimmune chronic disorder that affects your main organs, and has your body attacking itself when it should be defending you. Imagine living in a body that you can't trust sometimes. You don't have control over pain and the pain comes at the most inopportune moments. It's complete torture and I wouldn't wish it on my worst enemy.

During the time of my diagnoses I launched my digital magazine for female entrepreneurs. This was defiantly a major setback and has affected me as an entrepreneur in so many ways. There are days when I cannot put one foot in front of the other, or when I do not know if I am going or coming. Many days I am working from my bed because the pain is so intense that I cannot move. Furthermore, sometimes I have cancelled appointments and meetings because I just cannot physically or mentally deal and commit to them. That results in loss of business deals and opportunities. We know we all need money to live and do business, so that is a big setback. I began to seek the Lord concerning this and I found out that God promised me that He would take care of me (Isaiah 46).

Honestly, in what I saw, the diagnoses were a defeat. I am reminded of the late Dr. Maya Angelou and my favorite quote, "You will encounter many defeats, but you must not be defeated." In other words, the weapon of lupus may form but it will not prosper (Isaiah 54:17). It is a constant struggle. Every day I am saying, "God you promised me that **BY YOUR STRIPES I AM HEALED!**" (Isaiah 53:5). Though the symptoms do not show healing, it is a constant battle of believing the word of

God when I am constantly having symptoms of pain. Now you may say, how could you say that? Take a walk in my shoes and you'll see.

Now you must know that there is glory in my story. Where you are challenged is where your anointing is. NOW I have come to learn and understand that. God has this thorn in my flesh to bring healing to others. I must first go through it to testify about his healing power. I can't tell you God is a healer unless I have been sick and needed healing. I am testament of his healing power. Although I am fighting this lupus battle daily, I AM HEALED, BY HIS STRIPES!

CHAPTER 10

Speak Life Exercise

Another thing Julie Meyer said was, "The WORD heals." As you read in Latonya's phenomenal story, she spoke the word and life to her symptoms. Although the **physical** symptoms are there, she was living out Proverbs 18:21, King James Version (KJV), which states, "Death and life are in the power of the tongue; and they that love it shall eat the fruit thereof." She understands she is already healed according to Isaiah 53:5 and waiting on the manifestation of it to show up. What about you? What do you do in the meantime? Here's what you do. Annotate what lifestyle situation, symptom, habit, etc. you need to speak life into, or about which you can "sing the WORD":

_____

_____

_____

_____

_____

_____

_____

_____

_____

_____

_____

_____

_____

Latonya took control over her "meantime." She knew lupus patients should avoid certain foods. But she loves to cook soul food. Are there other options? Yes. Let's look at one. Veganism is a type of vegetarian diet that excludes meat, eggs, dairy products and all other animal-derived ingredients.

CHAPTER 11

Vegan Soul Food
By Chef Eboni Dionne
(Fort Worth, TX)

HOT WATER SWEET POTATO CORNBREAD

INGREDIENTS:

2 cups Cornmeal
1 sm-md Baked Sweet Potato
3/4 cup Aall-spelt flour
1 tsps Sea Salt
1/2 tsp baking soda
1 tbsp baking powder
1 tbsp raw organic cane sugar
3 tbsp Applesauce

DIRECTIONS
1. Mix together the cornmeal, flour, salt, baking powder, baking soda and sugar.
2. Stir in the applesauce and

mashed baked sweet potato.

3. Slowly add enough boiling water

until you have a thick batter that you can form into patties.

4. Form into patties and fry in hot oil in a heavy skillet

until golden

brown on both sides.

5. Serve immediately.

COLLARD GREENS

INGREDIENTS:

1-2 Bunches Collard Greens
1 Orange or Red Bell Pepper
1 Red Onion
1 Jalapeño Pepper
3-4 Cloves Garlic
Sweet Paprika
Sea Salt
Black Pepper
2 tbsps Olive Oil
1 tbsp White Truffle Oil (optional)

DIRECTIONS

1. Pick the greens and wash them until all the dirt is removed.

2. Give the greens a course chop. I like to make bite size pieces.

3. Slice the onions and peppers in bite size slivers. Give the garlic a nice chopping.

4. Heat a few tbsps. of olive oil. Olive oil has a very low smoke point so watch it closely; it won't take long to heat.

5. Add your peppers, onions and garlic. Season your veggies to your taste. Infusing your aromatics and oils with your seasonings gives a richer flavor to your food. Sauté your medley until the peppers begin to soften just a bit. It should take only a few minutes.

6. Add your cleaned, rinsed and dried greens. Add just a bit more seasoning to layer the flavors. Now sauté your greens on medium until they soften to being fork tender. This should take less than 10 minutes depending on the size of the pan and amount of greens.

7. Top off greens with white truffle oil once they are finished cooking.

8. Serve and eat as a side dish or a main course. This dish has been kid tested and mother approved!

LINDA D. LEE

CHAPTER 12

Book of Psalms Manifested

Julie Meyer, a guest on Sid Roth's It's Supernatural Show, shared a strategy to manifest healing in song. She suggested singing the book of Psalms. Since the book of Psalms are songs, we're used to reading them. It will feel different to learn how to "sing the WORD." You don't need any music. You don't need a choir. You don't even need a beat. Simply, pray for all clutter to be removed and a divine release to come forth. Be still, quiet your mind, and start "singing the word" from your belly, not your flesh. Meaning, let a melody flow out of you regardless of how it sounds to your natural ear. Singing the WORD will awaken your inner hearing with joy and sound delightful. There are 150 Psalms to choose from. However, Psalm 1-23 are listed here to quickly get you started in practical exercises to "sing the WORD" to your success. Psalms 91 and Psalms 103 have been added as special weapons.

Here is a little history on Psalms. It is divided into 5 books in the Hebrew Bible: Book 1 called the Genesis book (1-41); Book 2 called the Exodus book (42-72);

Book 3 called the Leviticus book (73-89); Book IV called the Numbers book (90-106, and Book V called the Deuteronomy book (107-150). Writers include: David, Asaph, the Sons of Korah, Solomon, Moses, Heman, Ethan, and 48 anonymous authors not named. The chief groups consist of: Alphabetic or Acrostic, Ethical, Hallelujah, Historical, Imprecatory, Messianic, Penitential, Songs of Ascent, (or Songs of Degrees), Suffering, and Thanksgiving. The various styles include: Didactic, Liturgical, Meditation, Praise & Devotion, and Prayer & Petition.[2]

Now practice...practice...practice singing the word to your healthy success.

....

Psalm 1 New King James Version (NKJV)

Psalms 1-23

The Way of the Righteous and the End of the Ungodly

[1] Blessed *is* the man
Who walks not in the counsel of the [a]ungodly,
Nor stands in the path of sinners,
Nor sits in the seat of the scornful;
[2] But his delight *is* in the law of the LORD,
And in His law he [b]meditates day and night.
[3] He shall be like a tree

Planted by the [c]rivers of water,
That brings forth its fruit in its season,
Whose leaf also shall not wither;
And whatever he does shall prosper.

4 The ungodly *are* not so,
But *are* like the chaff which the wind drives away.
5 Therefore the ungodly shall not stand in the judgment,
Nor sinners in the congregation of the righteous.

6 For the LORD knows the way of the righteous,
But the way of the ungodly shall perish.

Psalm 2 New King James Version (NKJV)

The Messiah's Triumph and Kingdom

1 Why do the [a]nations [b]rage,
And the people plot a [c]vain thing?
2 The kings of the earth set themselves,
And the rulers take counsel together,
Against the LORD and against His Anointed,[d] *saying,*
3 "Let us break Their bonds in pieces
And cast away Their cords from us."
4 He who sits in the heavens shall laugh;
The Lord shall hold them in derision.
5 Then He shall speak to them in His wrath,
And distress them in His deep displeasure:

[6] "Yet I have [e]set My King
[f]On My holy hill of Zion."
[7] "I will declare the [g]decree:
The LORD has said to Me,
'You *are* My Son,
Today I have begotten You.
[8] Ask of Me, and I will give *You*
The nations *for* Your inheritance,
And the ends of the earth *for* Your possession.
[9] You shall [h]break them with a rod of iron;
You shall dash them to pieces like a potter's vessel.' "
[10] Now therefore, be wise, O kings;
Be instructed, you judges of the earth.
[11] Serve the LORD with fear,
And rejoice with trembling.
[12] [i]Kiss the Son, lest [j]He be angry,
And you perish *in* the way,
When His wrath is kindled but a little.
Blessed *are* all those who put their trust in Him.

Psalm 3 New King James Version (NKJV)

The LORD Helps His Troubled People

A Psalm of David when he fled from Absalom his son.

[1] LORD, how they have increased who trouble me!
Many *are* they who rise up against me.
[2] Many *are* they who say of me,
" *There is* no help for him in God." *Selah*

[3] But You, O LORD, *are* a shield [a]for me,
My glory and the One who lifts up my head.
[4] I cried to the LORD with my voice,
And He heard me from His holy hill. *Selah*
[5] I lay down and slept;
I awoke, for the LORD sustained me.
[6] I will not be afraid of ten thousands of people
Who have set *themselves* against me all around.
[7] Arise, O LORD;
Save me, O my God!
For You have struck all my enemies on the cheekbone;
You have broken the teeth of the ungodly.
[8] Salvation *belongs* to the LORD.
Your blessing *is* upon Your people. *Selah*

Psalm 4 New King James Version (NKJV)

The Safety of the Faithful

To the [a]Chief Musician. With stringed instruments. A Psalm of David.

[1] Hear me when I call, O God of my righteousness!
You have relieved me in *my* distress;
[b]Have mercy on me, and hear my prayer.
[2] How long, O you sons of men,
Will you turn my glory to shame?
How long will you love worthlessness
And seek falsehood? *Selah*

³ But know that the LORD has [c]set apart for Himself him who is godly;

The LORD will hear when I call to Him.

⁴ Be[d] angry, and do not sin.

Meditate within your heart on your bed, and be still. *Selah*

⁵ Offer the sacrifices of righteousness,

And put your trust in the LORD.

⁶ *There are* many who say,

"Who will show us *any* good?"

LORD, lift up the light of Your countenance upon us.

⁷ You have put gladness in my heart,

More than in the season that their grain and wine increased.

⁸ I will both lie down in peace, and sleep;

For You alone, O LORD, make me dwell in safety.

Psalm 5 New King James Version (NKJV)

A Prayer for Guidance

To the Chief Musician. With [a]flutes. A Psalm of David.

¹ Give ear to my words, O LORD,

Consider my [b]meditation.

² Give heed to the voice of my cry,

My King and my God,

For to You I will pray.

³ My voice You shall hear in the morning, O LORD;

In the morning I will direct *it* to You,
And I will look up.
[4] For You *are* not a God who takes pleasure in
wickedness,
Nor shall evil [c]dwell with You.
[5] The boastful shall not stand in Your sight;
You hate all workers of iniquity.
[6] You shall destroy those who speak falsehood;
The LORD abhors the bloodthirsty and deceitful man.
[7] But as for me, I will come into Your house in the
multitude of Your mercy;
In fear of You I will worship toward [d]Your holy temple.
[8] Lead me, O LORD, in Your righteousness because of my
enemies;
Make Your way straight before my face.
[9] For *there is* no [e]faithfulness in their mouth;
Their inward part *is* destruction;
Their throat *is* an open tomb;
They flatter with their tongue.
[10] Pronounce them guilty, O God!
Let them fall by their own counsels;
Cast them out in the multitude of their transgressions,
For they have rebelled against You.
[11] But let all those rejoice who put their trust in You;
Let them ever shout for joy, because You [f]defend them;
Let those also who love Your name
Be joyful in You.
[12] For You, O LORD, will bless the righteous;
With favor You will surround him as *with* a shield.

Psalm 6 New King James Version (NKJV)

A Prayer of Faith in Time of Distress

To the Chief Musician. With stringed instruments. On [a]an eight-stringed harp. A Psalm of David.

[1] O LORD, do not rebuke me in Your anger,
Nor chasten me in Your hot displeasure.
[2] Have mercy on me, O LORD, for I *am* weak;
O LORD, heal me, for my bones are troubled.
[3] My soul also is greatly troubled;
But You, O LORD—how long?
[4] Return, O LORD, deliver me!
Oh, save me for Your mercies' sake!
[5] For in death *there is* no remembrance of You;
In the grave who will give You thanks?
[6] I am weary with my groaning;
[b]All night I make my bed swim;
I drench my couch with my tears.
[7] My eye wastes away because of grief;
It grows old because of all my enemies.
[8] Depart from me, all you workers of iniquity;
For the LORD has heard the voice of my weeping.
[9] The LORD has heard my supplication;
The LORD will receive my prayer.
[10] Let all my enemies be ashamed and greatly troubled;
Let them turn back *and* be ashamed suddenly.

Psalm 7 New King James Version (NKJV)

Prayer and Praise for Deliverance from Enemies

A Meditation[a] of David, which he sang to
the LORD concerning the words of Cush, a Benjamite.

1 O LORD my God, in You I put my trust;
Save me from all those who persecute me;
And deliver me,
2 Lest they tear me like a lion,
Rending *me* in pieces, while *there is* none to deliver.
3 O LORD my God, if I have done this:
If there is iniquity in my hands,
4 If I have repaid evil to him who was at peace with me,
Or have plundered my enemy without cause,
5 Let the enemy pursue me and overtake *me;*
Yes, let him trample my life to the earth,
And lay my honor in the dust. *Selah*
6 Arise, O LORD, in Your anger;
Lift Yourself up because of the rage of my enemies;
Rise up [b]for me *to* the judgment You have commanded!
7 So the congregation of the peoples shall surround You;
For their sakes, therefore, return on high.
8 The LORD shall judge the peoples;
Judge me, O LORD, according to my righteousness,
And according to my integrity within me.

[9] Oh, let the wickedness of the wicked come to an end,
But establish the just;
For the righteous God tests the hearts and [c]minds.
[10] [d]My defense *is* of God,
Who saves the upright in heart.
[11] God *is* a just judge,
And God is angry *with the wicked* every day.
[12] If he does not turn back,
He will sharpen His sword;
He bends His bow and makes it ready.
[13] He also prepares for Himself instruments of death;
He makes His arrows into fiery shafts.
[14] Behold, *the wicked* brings forth iniquity;
Yes, he conceives trouble and brings forth falsehood.
[15] He made a pit and dug it out,
And has fallen into the ditch *which* he made.
[16] His trouble shall return upon his own head,
And his violent dealing shall come down on [e]his own
crown.
[17] I will praise the LORD according to His righteousness,
And will sing praise to the name of the LORD Most High.

Psalm 8 New King James Version (NKJV)

The Glory of the LORD in Creation

To the Chief Musician. [a]On the instrument of Gath. A Psalm of David.

¹O LORD, our Lord,
How excellent *is* Your name in all the earth,
Who have set Your glory above the heavens!
² Out of the mouth of babes and nursing infants
You have [b]ordained strength,
Because of Your enemies,
That You may silence the enemy and the avenger.
³ When I consider Your heavens, the work of Your fingers,
The moon and the stars, which You have ordained,
⁴ What is man that You are mindful of him,
And the son of man that You visit[c] him?
⁵ For You have made him a little lower than [d]the angels,
And You have crowned him with glory and honor.
⁶ You have made him to have dominion over the works of Your hands;
You have put all *things* under his feet,
⁷ All sheep and oxen—
Even the beasts of the field,
⁸ The birds of the air,
And the fish of the sea
That pass through the paths of the seas.
⁹ O LORD, our Lord,
How excellent *is* Your name in all the earth!

63

Psalm 9 New King James Version (NKJV)

Prayer and Thanksgiving for the LORD's Righteous Judgments

To the Chief Musician. To the tune of [a] *"Death of the Son." A Psalm of David.*

[1] I will praise *You,* O LORD, with my whole heart;
I will tell of all Your marvelous works.
[2] I will be glad and rejoice in You;
I will sing praise to Your name, O Most High.
[3] When my enemies turn back,
They shall fall and perish at Your presence.
[4] For You have maintained my right and my cause;
You sat on the throne judging in righteousness.
[5] You have rebuked the [b]nations,
You have destroyed the wicked;
You have blotted out their name forever and ever.
[6] O enemy, destructions are finished forever!
And you have destroyed cities;
Even their memory has perished.
[7] But the LORD shall endure forever;
He has prepared His throne for judgment.
[8] He shall judge the world in righteousness,
And He shall administer judgment for the peoples in uprightness.
[9] The LORD also will be a refuge[c] for the oppressed,
A refuge in times of trouble.
[10] And those who know Your name will put their trust in

You;

For You, LORD, have not forsaken those who seek You.

[11] Sing praises to the LORD, who dwells in Zion!

Declare His deeds among the people.

[12] When He avenges blood, He remembers them;

He does not forget the cry of the [d]humble.

[13] Have mercy on me, O LORD!

Consider my trouble from those who hate me,

You who lift me up from the gates of death,

[14] That I may tell of all Your praise

In the gates of [e]the daughter of Zion.

I will rejoice in Your salvation.

[15] The [f]nations have sunk down in the pit *which* they made;

In the net which they hid, their own foot is caught.

[16] The LORD is known *by* the judgment He executes;

The wicked is snared in the work of his own hands.

Meditation.[g] *Selah*

[17] The wicked shall be turned into hell,

And all the [h]nations that forget God.

[18] For the needy shall not always be forgotten;

The expectation of the poor shall *not* perish forever.

[19] Arise, O LORD,

Do not let man prevail;

Let the [i]nations be judged in Your sight.

[20] Put them in fear, O LORD,

That the [i]nations may know themselves *to be*

but men. *Selah*

Psalm 10 New King James Version (NKJV)

A Song of Confidence in God's Triumph over Evil

[1]Why do You stand afar off, O LORD?
Why do You hide in times of trouble?
[2] The wicked in *his* pride [a]persecutes the poor;
Let them be caught in the plots which they have devised.
[3] For the wicked boasts of his heart's desire;
[b]He blesses the greedy *and* renounces the LORD.
[4] The wicked in his proud countenance does not
seek *God;*
[c]God *is* in none of his thoughts.
[5] His ways [d]are always prospering;
Your judgments *are* far above, out of his sight;
As for all his enemies, he sneers at them.
[6] He has said in his heart, "I shall not be moved;
I shall never be in adversity."
[7] His mouth is full of cursing and deceit and oppression;
Under his tongue *is* trouble and iniquity.
[8] He sits in the lurking places of the villages;
In the secret places he murders the innocent;
His eyes are secretly fixed on the helpless.
[9] He lies in wait secretly, as a lion in his den;
He lies in wait to catch the poor;
He catches the poor when he draws him into his net.
[10] So [e]he crouches, he lies low,
That the helpless may fall by his [f]strength.
[11] He has said in his heart,
"God has forgotten;

He hides His face;
He will never see."
[12] Arise, O LORD!
O God, lift up Your hand!
Do not forget the humble.
[13] Why do the wicked renounce God?
He has said in his heart,
"You will not require *an account*."
[14] But You have seen, for You observe trouble and grief,
To repay *it* by Your hand.
The helpless commits[g] himself to You;
You are the helper of the fatherless.
[15] Break the arm of the wicked and the evil *man;*
Seek out his wickedness *until* You find none.
[16] The LORD *is* King forever and ever;
The nations have perished out of His land.
[17] LORD, You have heard the desire of the humble;
You will prepare their heart;
You will cause Your ear to hear,
[18] To [h]do justice to the fatherless and the oppressed,
That the man of the earth may [i]oppress no more.

Psalm 11 New King James Version (NKJV)

Faith in the LORD's Righteousness

To the Chief Musician. A Psalm *of David.*

[1]In the LORD I put my trust;
How can you say to my soul,

"Flee *as* a bird to your mountain"?
² For look! The wicked bend *their* bow,
They make ready their arrow on the string,
That they may shoot [a]secretly at the upright in heart.
³ If the foundations are destroyed,
What can the righteous do?
⁴ The LORD *is* in His holy temple,
The LORD's throne *is* in heaven;
His eyes behold,
His eyelids test the sons of men.
⁵ The LORD tests the righteous,
But the wicked and the one who loves violence His soul hates.
⁶ Upon the wicked He will rain coals;
Fire and brimstone and a burning wind
Shall be [b]the portion of their cup.
⁷ For the LORD *is* righteous,
He loves righteousness;
[c]His countenance beholds the upright.

Psalm 12 New King James Version (NKJV)

Man's Treachery and God's Constancy

To the Chief Musician. On [a]an eight-stringed harp. A Psalm of David.

¹Help,[b] LORD, for the godly man ceases!
For the faithful disappear from among the sons of men.

2 They speak idly everyone with his neighbor;

With flattering lips *and* [c]a double heart they speak.

3 May the LORD [d]cut off all flattering lips,

And the tongue that speaks [e]proud things,

4 Who have said,

"With our tongue we will prevail;

Our lips *are* our own;

Who *is* lord over us?"

5 "For the oppression of the poor, for the sighing of the needy,

Now I will arise," says the LORD;

"I will set *him* in the safety for which he yearns."

6 The words of the LORD *are* pure words,

Like silver tried in a furnace of earth,

Purified seven times.

7 You shall keep them, O LORD,

You shall preserve them from this generation forever.

8 The wicked prowl on every side,

When vileness is exalted among the sons of men.

Psalm 13 New King James Version (NKJV)

Trust in the Salvation of the LORD

To the Chief Musician. A Psalm of David.

1 How long, O LORD? Will You forget me forever?

How long will You hide Your face from me?

2 How long shall I take counsel in my soul,

Having sorrow in my heart daily?
How long will my enemy be exalted over me?
³ Consider *and* hear me, O LORD my God;
Enlighten my eyes,
Lest I sleep the *sleep of* death;
⁴ Lest my enemy say,
"I have prevailed against him";
Lest those who trouble me rejoice when I am moved.
⁵ But I have trusted in Your mercy;
My heart shall rejoice in Your salvation.
⁶ I will sing to the LORD,
Because He has dealt bountifully with me.

Psalm 14 New King James Version (NKJV)

Folly of the Godless, and God's Final Triumph

To the Chief Musician. A Psalm *of David.*

¹The fool has said in his heart,
"*There is* no God."
They are corrupt,
They have done abominable works,
There is none who does good.
² The LORD looks down from heaven upon the children
of men,
To see if there are any who understand, who seek God.
³ They have all turned aside,
They have together become corrupt;

There is none who does good,
No, not one.
⁴ Have all the workers of iniquity no knowledge,
Who eat up my people *as* they eat bread,
And do not call on the LORD?
⁵ There they are in great fear,
For God *is* with the generation of the righteous.
⁶ You shame the counsel of the poor,
But the LORD *is* his refuge.
⁷ Oh,[a] that the salvation of Israel *would come* out of Zion!
When the LORD brings back [b]the captivity of His people,
Let Jacob rejoice *and* Israel be glad.

Psalm 15 New King James Version (NKJV)

The Character of Those Who May Dwell with the LORD

A Psalm of David.

¹LORD, who may [a]abide in Your tabernacle?
Who may dwell in Your holy hill?
² He who walks uprightly,
And works righteousness,
And speaks the truth in his heart;
³ He *who* does not backbite with his tongue,
Nor does evil to his neighbor,
Nor does he [b]take up a reproach against his friend;
⁴ In whose eyes a vile person is despised,
But he honors those who fear the LORD;
He *who* swears to his own hurt and does not change;

⁵He *who* does not put out his money at usury,
Nor does he take a bribe against the innocent.
He who does these *things* shall never be moved.

Psalm 16 New King James Version (NKJV)

The Hope of the Faithful, and the Messiah's Victory

A Michtam of David.

¹Preserve[a] me, O God, for in You I put my trust.
² *O my soul,* you have said to the LORD,
"You *are* my Lord,
My goodness is nothing apart from You."
³As for the saints who *are* on the earth,
"They are the excellent ones, in whom is all my delight."
⁴Their sorrows shall be multiplied who
hasten *after* another *god;*
Their drink offerings of blood I will not offer,
Nor take up their names on my lips.
⁵O LORD, *You are* the portion of my inheritance and my cup;
You [b]maintain my lot.
⁶The lines have fallen to me in pleasant *places;*
Yes, I have a good inheritance.
⁷I will bless the LORD who has given me counsel;
My [c]heart also instructs me in the night seasons.
⁸I have set the LORD always before me;
Because *He is* at my right hand I shall not be moved.

[9] Therefore my heart is glad, and my glory rejoices;
My flesh also will [d]rest in hope.
[10] For You will not leave my soul in [e]Sheol,
Nor will You allow Your Holy One to [f]see corruption.
[11] You will show me the path of life;
In Your presence *is* fullness of joy;
At Your right hand *are* pleasures forevermore.

Psalm 17 New King James Version (NKJV)

Prayer with Confidence in Final Salvation

A Prayer of David.

[1] Hear a just cause, O LORD,
Attend to my cry;
Give ear to my prayer *which is* not from deceitful lips.
[2] Let my vindication come from Your presence;
Let Your eyes look on the things that are upright.
[3] You have tested my heart;
You have visited *me* in the night;
You have [a]tried me and have found [b]nothing;
I have purposed that my mouth shall not transgress.
[4] Concerning the works of men,
By the word of Your lips,
I have kept away from the paths of the destroyer.
[5] Uphold my steps in Your paths,
That my footsteps may not slip.
[6] I have called upon You, for You will hear me, O God;
Incline Your ear to me, *and* hear my speech.

[7] Show Your marvelous lovingkindness by Your right
hand,

O You who [c]save those who trust *in You*
From those who rise up *against them.*
[8] Keep me as the [d]apple of Your eye;
Hide me under the shadow of Your wings,
[9] From the wicked who oppress me,
From my deadly enemies who surround me.
[10] They have closed up their fat *hearts;*
With their mouths they speak proudly.
[11] They have now surrounded us in our steps;
They have set their eyes, crouching down to the earth,
[12] As a lion is eager to tear his prey,
And like a young lion lurking in secret places.
[13] Arise, O LORD,
Confront him, cast him down;
Deliver my life from the wicked with Your sword,
[14] With Your hand from men, O LORD,
From men of the world *who have* their portion in *this* life,
And whose belly You fill with Your hidden treasure.
They are satisfied with children,
And leave the rest of their *possession* for their babes.
[15] As for me, I will see Your face in righteousness;
I shall be satisfied when I awake in Your likeness.

Psalm 18 New King James Version (NKJV)

God the Sovereign Savior

To the Chief Musician. A Psalm of David the servant of the LORD, who spoke to the LORD the words of this song on the day that the LORD delivered him from the hand of all his enemies and from the hand of Saul. And he said:

¹I will love You, O LORD, my strength.
²The LORD is my rock and my fortress and my deliverer;
My God, my [a]strength, in whom I will trust;
My shield and the [b]horn of my salvation, my stronghold.
³I will call upon the LORD, *who is worthy* to be praised;
So shall I be saved from my enemies.
⁴The pangs of death surrounded me,
And the floods of [c]ungodliness made me afraid.
⁵The sorrows of Sheol surrounded me;
The snares of death confronted me.
⁶In my distress I called upon the LORD,
And cried out to my God;
He heard my voice from His temple,
And my cry came before Him, *even* to His ears.
⁷Then the earth shook and trembled;
The foundations of the hills also quaked and were shaken,
Because He was angry.
⁸Smoke went up from His nostrils,
And devouring fire from His mouth;
Coals were kindled by it.
⁹He bowed the heavens also, and came down
With darkness under His feet.
¹⁰And He rode upon a cherub, and flew;

He flew upon the wings of the wind.

¹¹ He made darkness His secret place;

His canopy around Him *was* dark waters

And thick clouds of the skies.

¹² From the brightness before Him,

His thick clouds passed with hailstones and coals of fire.

¹³ The LORD thundered from heaven,

And the Most High uttered His voice,

[d]Hailstones and coals of fire.

¹⁴ He sent out His arrows and scattered [e]the foe,

Lightnings in abundance, and He vanquished them.

¹⁵ Then the channels of the sea were seen,

The foundations of the world were uncovered

At Your rebuke, O LORD,

At the blast of the breath of Your nostrils.

¹⁶ He sent from above, He took me;

He drew me out of many waters.

¹⁷ He delivered me from my strong enemy,

From those who hated me,

For they were too strong for me.

¹⁸ They confronted me in the day of my calamity,

But the LORD was my support.

¹⁹ He also brought me out into a broad place;

He delivered me because He delighted in me.

²⁰ The LORD rewarded me according to my righteousness;

According to the cleanness of my hands

He has recompensed me.

²¹ For I have kept the ways of the LORD,

And have not wickedly departed from my God.

²² For all His judgments *were* before me,

And I did not put away His statutes from me.

²³ I was also blameless ^[i]before Him,

And I kept myself from my iniquity.

²⁴ Therefore the LORD has recompensed me according to my righteousness,

According to the cleanness of my hands in His sight.

²⁵ With the merciful You will show Yourself merciful;

With a blameless man You will show Yourself blameless;

²⁶ With the pure You will show Yourself pure;

And with the devious You will show Yourself shrewd.

²⁷ For You will save the humble people,

But will bring down haughty looks.

²⁸ For You will light my lamp;

The LORD my God will enlighten my darkness.

²⁹ For by You I can ^[g]run against a troop,

By my God I can leap over a wall.

³⁰ *As for* God, His way *is* perfect;

The word of the LORD is ^[h]proven;

He *is* a shield to all who trust in Him.

³¹ For who *is* God, except the LORD?

And who *is* a rock, except our God?

³² *It is* God who arms me with strength,

And makes my way perfect.

³³ He makes my feet like the *feet of* deer,

And sets me on my high places.

³⁴ He teaches my hands to make war,

So that my arms can bend a bow of bronze.

³⁵ You have also given me the shield of Your salvation;
Your right hand has held me up,
Your gentleness has made me great.
³⁶ You enlarged my path under me,
So my feet did not slip.
³⁷ I have pursued my enemies and overtaken them;
Neither did I turn back again till they were destroyed.
³⁸ I have wounded them,
So that they could not rise;
They have fallen under my feet.
³⁹ For You have armed me with strength for the battle;
You have [i]subdued under me those who rose up against
me.
⁴⁰ You have also given me the necks of my enemies,
So that I destroyed those who hated me.
⁴¹ They cried out, but *there was* none to save;
Even to the LORD, but He did not answer them.
⁴² Then I beat them as fine as the dust before the wind;
I cast them out like dirt in the streets.
⁴³ You have delivered me from the strivings of the people;
You have made me the head of the [j]nations;
A people I have not known shall serve me.
⁴⁴ As soon as they hear of me they obey me;
The foreigners [k]submit to me.
⁴⁵ The foreigners fade away,
And come frightened from their hideouts.
⁴⁶ The LORD lives!
Blessed *be* my Rock!
Let the God of my salvation be exalted.

⁴⁷ *It is* God who avenges me,

And subdues the peoples under me;

⁴⁸ He delivers me from my enemies.

You also lift me up above those who rise against me;

You have delivered me from the violent man.

⁴⁹ Therefore I will give thanks to You, O LORD, among the [l]Gentiles,

And sing praises to Your name.

⁵⁰ Great deliverance He gives to His king,

And shows mercy to His anointed,

To David and his [m]descendants forevermore.

Psalm 19 New King James Version (NKJV)

The Perfect Revelation of the LORD

To the Chief Musician. A Psalm of David.

¹The heavens declare the glory of God;

And the firmament[a] shows [b]His handiwork.

² Day unto day utters speech,

And night unto night reveals knowledge.

³ *There is* no speech nor language

Where their voice is not heard.

⁴ Their [c]line has gone out through all the earth,

And their words to the end of the world.

In them He has set a [d]tabernacle for the sun,

⁵ Which *is* like a bridegroom coming out of his chamber,

And rejoices like a strong man to run its race.

⁶ Its rising *is* from one end of heaven,

And its circuit to the other end;
And there is nothing hidden from its heat.
[7] The law of the LORD *is* perfect, [c]converting the soul;
The testimony of the LORD *is* sure, making wise the simple;
[8] The statutes of the LORD *are* right, rejoicing the heart;
The commandment of the LORD *is* pure, enlightening the eyes;
[9] The fear of the LORD *is* clean, enduring forever;
The judgments of the LORD *are* true *and* righteous altogether.
[10] More to be desired *are they* than gold,
Yea, than much fine gold;
Sweeter also than honey and the [f]honeycomb.
[11] Moreover by them Your servant is warned,
And in keeping them *there is* great reward.
[12] Who can understand *his* errors?
Cleanse me from secret *faults.*
[13] Keep back Your servant also from presumptuous *sins;*
Let them not have dominion over me.
Then I shall be blameless,
And I shall be innocent of [g]great transgression.
[14] Let the words of my mouth and the meditation of my heart
Be acceptable in Your sight,
O LORD, my [h]strength and my Redeemer.

Psalm 20 New King James Version (NKJV)

The Assurance of God's Saving Work

To the Chief Musician. A Psalm of David.

[1]May the LORD answer you in the day of trouble;
May the name of the God of Jacob [a]defend you;
[2] May He send you help from the sanctuary,
And strengthen you out of Zion;
[3] May He remember all your offerings,
And accept your burnt sacrifice. *Selah*
[4] May He grant you according to your heart's *desire,*
And fulfill all your [b]purpose.
[5] We will rejoice in your salvation,
And in the name of our God we will set up *our* banners!
May the LORD fulfill all your petitions.
[6] Now I know that the LORD saves His [c]anointed;
He will answer him from His holy heaven
With the saving strength of His right hand.
[7] Some *trust* in chariots, and some in horses;
But we will remember the name of the LORD our God.
[8] They have bowed down and fallen;
But we have risen and stand upright.
[9] Save, LORD!
May the King answer us when we call.

Psalm 21 New King James Version (NKJV)

Joy in the Salvation of the LORD

To the Chief Musician. A Psalm of David.

¹The king shall have joy in Your strength, O LORD;
And in Your salvation how greatly shall he rejoice!
² You have given him his heart's desire,
And have not withheld the request of his lips. *Selah*
³ For You meet him with the blessings of goodness;
You set a crown of pure gold upon his head.
⁴ He asked life from You, *and* You gave *it* to him—
Length of days forever and ever.
⁵ His glory *is* great in Your salvation;
Honor and majesty You have placed upon him.
⁶ For You have made him most blessed forever;
You have made him [a]exceedingly glad with Your
presence.
⁷ For the king trusts in the LORD,
And through the mercy of the Most High he shall not
be [b]moved.
⁸ Your hand will find all Your enemies;
Your right hand will find those who hate You.
⁹ You shall make them as a fiery oven in the time of Your
anger;
The LORD shall swallow them up in His wrath,
And the fire shall devour them.
¹⁰ Their offspring You shall destroy from the earth,
And their [c]descendants from among the sons of men.
¹¹ For they intended evil against You;

They devised a plot *which* they are not able *to perform.*
¹²Therefore You will make them turn their back;
You will make ready *Your arrows* on Your string toward their faces.
¹³Be exalted, O LORD, in Your own strength!
We will sing and praise Your power.

Psalm 22 New King James Version (NKJV)

The Suffering, Praise, and Posterity of the Messiah

To the Chief Musician. Set to [a]*"The Deer of the Dawn."
A Psalm of David.*

¹My God, My God, why have You forsaken Me?
Why are You so far from helping Me,
And from the words of My groaning?
²O My God, I cry in the daytime, but You do not hear;
And in the night season, and am not silent.
³But You *are* holy,
Enthroned in the praises of Israel.
⁴Our fathers trusted in You;
They trusted, and You delivered them.
⁵They cried to You, and were delivered;
They trusted in You, and were not ashamed.
⁶But I *am* a worm, and no man;
A reproach of men, and despised by the people.
⁷All those who see Me ridicule Me;
They [b]shoot out the lip, they shake the head, *saying,*

8 "He [c]trusted in the LORD, let Him rescue Him;
Let Him deliver Him, since He delights in Him!"
9 But You *are* He who took Me out of the womb;
You made Me trust *while* on My mother's breasts.
10 I was cast upon You from birth.
From My mother's womb
You *have been* My God.
11 Be not far from Me,
For trouble *is* near;
For *there is* none to help.
12 Many bulls have surrounded Me;
Strong *bulls* of Bashan have encircled Me.
13 They [d]gape at Me *with* their mouths,
Like a raging and roaring lion.
14 I am poured out like water,
And all My bones are out of joint;
My heart is like wax;
It has melted [e]within Me.
15 My strength is dried up like a potsherd,
And My tongue clings to My jaws;
You have brought Me to the dust of death.
16 For dogs have surrounded Me;
The congregation of the wicked has enclosed Me.
They[f] pierced My hands and My feet;
17 I can count all My bones.
They look *and* stare at Me.
18 They divide My garments among them,
And for My clothing they cast lots.

¹⁹ But You, O L<small>ORD</small>, do not be far from Me;
O My Strength, hasten to help Me!
²⁰ Deliver Me from the sword,
My^[g] precious *life* from the power of the dog.
²¹ Save Me from the lion's mouth
And from the horns of the wild oxen!
You have answered Me.
²² I will declare Your name to My brethren;
In the midst of the assembly I will praise You.
²³ You who fear the L<small>ORD</small>, praise Him!
All you ^[h]descendants of Jacob, glorify Him,
And fear Him, all you offspring of Israel!
²⁴ For He has not despised nor abhorred the affliction of
the afflicted;
Nor has He hidden His face from Him;
But when He cried to Him, He heard.
²⁵ My praise *shall be* of You in the great assembly;
I will pay My vows before those who fear Him.
²⁶ The poor shall eat and be satisfied;
Those who seek Him will praise the L<small>ORD</small>.
Let your heart live forever!
²⁷ All the ends of the world
Shall remember and turn to the L<small>ORD</small>,
And all the families of the ^[i]nations
Shall worship before ^[j]You.
²⁸ For the kingdom *is* the L<small>ORD</small>'s,
And He rules over the nations.
²⁹ All the prosperous of the earth
Shall eat and worship;

All those who go down to [k]the dust
Shall bow before Him,
Even he who cannot keep himself alive.
30 A posterity shall serve Him.
It will be recounted of the Lord to the *next* generation,
31 They will come and declare His righteousness to a
people who will be born,
That He has done *this*.

Psalm 23 New King James Version (NKJV)

The LORD the Shepherd of His People

A Psalm of David.

1The LORD *is* my shepherd;
I shall not [a]want.
2 He makes me to lie down in [b]green pastures;
He leads me beside the [c]still waters.
3 He restores my soul;
He leads me in the paths of righteousness
For His name's sake.
4 Yea, though I walk through the valley of the shadow of
death,
I will fear no evil;
For You *are* with me;
Your rod and Your staff, they comfort me.
5 You prepare a table before me in the presence of my
enemies;
You anoint my head with oil;

My cup runs over.
[6] Surely goodness and mercy shall follow me
All the days of my life;
And I will [d]dwell in the house of the LORD
[e]Forever.

SPECIAL WEAPONS

Psalm 91 New King James Version (NKJV) (The Prayer of Protection)

Safety of Abiding in the Presence of God

[1]He who dwells in the secret place of the Most High
Shall abide under the shadow of the Almighty.
[2] I will say of the LORD, "*He is* my refuge and my fortress;
My God, in Him I will trust."
[3] Surely He shall deliver you from the snare of the [a]fowler
And from the perilous pestilence.
[4] He shall cover you with His feathers,
And under His wings you shall take refuge;
His truth *shall be your* shield and [b]buckler.
[5] You shall not be afraid of the terror by night,
Nor of the arrow *that* flies by day,
[6] *Nor* of the pestilence *that* walks in darkness,
Nor of the destruction *that* lays waste at noonday.
[7] A thousand may fall at your side,
And ten thousand at your right hand;
But it shall not come near you.

⁸ Only with your eyes shall you look,
And see the reward of the wicked.
⁹ Because you have made the L<small>ORD</small>, *who is* my refuge,
Even the Most High, your dwelling place,
¹⁰ No evil shall befall you,
Nor shall any plague come near your dwelling;
¹¹ For He shall give His angels charge over you,
To keep you in all your ways.
¹² In *their* hands they shall [c]bear you up,
Lest you [d]dash your foot against a stone.
¹³ You shall tread upon the lion and the cobra,
The young lion and the serpent you shall trample underfoot.
¹⁴ "Because he has set his love upon Me, therefore I will deliver him;
I will [e]set him on high, because he has known My name.
¹⁵ He shall call upon Me, and I will answer him;
I *will be* with him in trouble;
I will deliver him and honor him.
¹⁶ With [f]long life I will satisfy him,
And show him My salvation."

Psalm 103 New King James Version (NKJV) (The Benefit Package)

Praise for the L<small>ORD</small>'s Mercies

A Psalm *of David.*

¹Bless the LORD, O my soul;
And all that is within me, *bless* His holy name!
² Bless the LORD, O my soul,
And forget not all His benefits:
³ Who forgives all your iniquities,
Who heals all your diseases,
⁴ Who redeems your life from destruction,
Who crowns you with lovingkindness and tender mercies,
⁵ Who satisfies your mouth with good *things,*
So that your youth is renewed like the eagle's.
⁶ The LORD executes righteousness
And justice for all who are oppressed.
⁷ He made known His ways to Moses,
His acts to the children of Israel.
⁸ The LORD *is* merciful and gracious,
Slow to anger, and abounding in mercy.
⁹ He will not always strive *with us,*
Nor will He keep *His anger* forever.
¹⁰ He has not dealt with us according to our sins,
Nor punished us according to our iniquities.
¹¹ For as the heavens are high above the earth,
So great is His mercy toward those who fear Him;
¹² As far as the east is from the west,
So far has He removed our transgressions from us.
¹³ As a father pities *his* children,
So the LORD pities those who fear Him.
¹⁴ For He [a]knows our frame;
He remembers that we *are* dust.

[15] *As for* man, his days *are* like grass;

As a flower of the field, so he flourishes.

[16] For the wind passes over it, and it is [b]gone,

And its place remembers it no more.

[17] But the mercy of the LORD *is* from everlasting to everlasting

On those who fear Him,

And His righteousness to children's children,

[18] To such as keep His covenant,

And to those who remember His commandments to do them.

[19] The LORD has established His throne in heaven,

And His kingdom rules over all.

[20] Bless the LORD, you His angels,

Who excel in strength, who do His word,

Heeding the voice of His word.

[21] Bless the LORD, all *you* His hosts,

You [c]ministers of His, who do His pleasure.

[22] Bless the LORD, all His works,

In all places of His dominion.

Bless the LORD, O my soul!

CHAPTER 13

FOOTNOTES

1. & 2. Martin, Lee, Professor Dr. "Books of Psalms."
Integrity Seminary. Red Oak, Texas, 2019. Lecture.

a. Psalm 1:1 *wicked*
b. Psalm 1:2 *ponders* by talking to himself
c. Psalm 1:3 *channels*

a. Psalm 2:1 *Gentiles*
b. Psalm 2:1 *throng tumultuously*
c. Psalm 2:1 *worthless* or *empty*
d. Psalm 2:2 Christ, Commissioned One,
Heb. *Messiah*
e. Psalm 2:6 Lit. *installed*
f. Psalm 2:6 Lit. *Upon Zion, the hill of My holiness*
g. Psalm 2:7 Or *decree of the LORD: He said to Me*
h. Psalm 2:9 So with MT, Tg.; LXX, Syr.,
Vg. *rule* (cf. Rev. 2:27)
i. Psalm 2:12 LXX, Vg. *Embrace
discipline;* Tg. *Receive instruction*
j. Psalm 2:12 LXX *the LORD*

a. Psalm 3:3 Lit. *around*

a. Psalm 4:1 *Choir Director*
b. Psalm 4:1 *Be gracious to me*
c. Psalm 4:3 Many Heb. mss., LXX, Tg., Vg. *made
wonderful*

d. <u>Psalm 4:4</u> Lit. *Tremble* or *Be agitated*

a. <u>Psalm 5:1</u> Heb. *nehiloth*
b. <u>Psalm 5:1</u> Lit. *groaning*
c. <u>Psalm 5:4</u> Lit. *sojourn*
d. <u>Psalm 5:7</u> Lit. *the temple of Your holiness*
e. <u>Psalm 5:9</u> *uprightness*
f. <u>Psalm 5:11</u> *protect,* lit. *cover*

a. <u>Psalm 6:1</u> Heb. *sheminith*
b. <u>Psalm 6:6</u> Or *Every night*

a. <u>Psalm 7:1</u> Heb. *Shiggaion*
b. <u>Psalm 7:6</u> So with MT, Tg., Vg.; LXX *O LORD my God*
c. <u>Psalm 7:9</u> Lit. *kidneys,* the most secret part of man
d. <u>Psalm 7:10</u> Lit. *My shield is upon God*
e. <u>Psalm 7:16</u> The crown of his own head

a. <u>Psalm 8:1</u> Heb. *Al Gittith*
b. <u>Psalm 8:2</u> *established*
c. <u>Psalm 8:4</u> *give attention to* or *care for*
d. <u>Psalm 8:5</u> Heb. *Elohim, God;* LXX, Syr., Tg., Jewish tradition *angels*

a. <u>Psalm 9:1</u> Heb. *Muth Labben*
b. <u>Psalm 9:5</u> *Gentiles*
c. <u>Psalm 9:9</u> Lit. *secure height*
d. <u>Psalm 9:12</u> *afflicted*
e. <u>Psalm 9:14</u> Jerusalem
f. <u>Psalm 9:15</u> *Gentiles*
g. <u>Psalm 9:16</u> Heb. *Higgaion*
h. <u>Psalm 9:17</u> *Gentiles*
i. <u>Psalm 9:19</u> *Gentiles*

j. Psalm 9:20 *Gentiles*

a. Psalm 10:2 *hotly pursues*
b. Psalm 10:3 Or *The greedy man curses and spurns the LORD*
c. Psalm 10:4 Or *All his thoughts are, "There is no God"*
d. Psalm 10:5 Lit. *are strong*
e. Psalm 10:10 Or *he is crushed, is bowed*
f. Psalm 10:10 Or *mighty ones*
g. Psalm 10:14 Lit. *leaves,* entrusts
h. Psalm 10:18 *vindicate*
i. Psalm 10:18 *terrify*

a. Psalm 11:2 Lit. *in darkness*
b. Psalm 11:6 Their allotted portion or serving
c. Psalm 11:7 Or *The upright beholds His countenance*

a. Psalm 12:1 Heb. *sheminith*
b. Psalm 12:1 *Save*
c. Psalm 12:2 An inconsistent mind
d. Psalm 12:3 *destroy*
e. Psalm 12:3 *great*

a. Psalm 14:7 Lit. *Who will give out of Zion the salvation of Israel?*
b. Psalm 14:7 Or *His captive people*

a. Psalm 15:1 *sojourn*
b. Psalm 15:3 *receive*

a. Psalm 16:1 *Watch over*
b. Psalm 16:5 Lit. *uphold*

c. <u>Psalm 16:7</u> Mind, lit. *kidneys*
d. <u>Psalm 16:9</u> Or *dwell securely*
e. <u>Psalm 16:10</u> The abode of the dead
f. <u>Psalm 16:10</u> *undergo*

a. <u>Psalm 17:3</u> *examined*
b. <u>Psalm 17:3</u> Nothing evil
c. <u>Psalm 17:7</u> *deliver*
d. <u>Psalm 17:8</u> *pupil*

a. <u>Psalm 18:2</u> Lit. *rock*
b. <u>Psalm 18:2</u> Strength
c. <u>Psalm 18:4</u> Lit. *Belial*
d. <u>Psalm 18:13</u> So with MT, Tg., Vg.; a few Heb. mss., LXX omit *Hailstones and coals of fire*
e. <u>Psalm 18:14</u> Lit. *them*
f. <u>Psalm 18:23</u> *with*
g. <u>Psalm 18:29</u> Or *run through*
h. <u>Psalm 18:30</u> Lit. *refined*
i. <u>Psalm 18:39</u> Lit. *caused to bow*
j. <u>Psalm 18:43</u> *Gentiles*
k. <u>Psalm 18:44</u> *feign submission*
l. <u>Psalm 18:49</u> *nations*
m. <u>Psalm 18:50</u> Lit. *seed*

a. <u>Psalm 19:1</u> *expanse* of heaven
b. <u>Psalm 19:1</u> *the work of His hands*
c. <u>Psalm 19:4</u> LXX, Syr., Vg. *sound;* Tg. *business*
d. <u>Psalm 19:4</u> *tent*
e. <u>Psalm 19:7</u> *restoring*
f. <u>Psalm 19:10</u> *honey in the combs*
g. <u>Psalm 19:13</u> Or *much*
h. <u>Psalm 19:14</u> Lit. *rock*

a. <u>Psalm 20:1</u> Lit. *set you on high*
b. <u>Psalm 20:4</u> *counsel*
c. <u>Psalm 20:6</u> Commissioned one, Heb. *messiah*

a. <u>Psalm 21:6</u> Lit. *joyful with gladness*
b. <u>Psalm 21:7</u> *shaken*
c. <u>Psalm 21:10</u> Lit. *seed*

a. <u>Psalm 22:1</u> Heb. *Aijeleth Hashahar*
b. <u>Psalm 22:7</u> Show contempt with their mouth
c. <u>Psalm 22:8</u> LXX, Syr., Vg. *hoped;* Tg. *praised*
d. <u>Psalm 22:13</u> Lit. *have opened their mouths at Me*
e. <u>Psalm 22:14</u> Lit. *in the midst of My bowels*
f. <u>Psalm 22:16</u> So with some Heb. mss., LXX, Syr., Vg.; MT *Like a lion* instead of *They pierced*
g. <u>Psalm 22:20</u> Lit. *My only one*
h. <u>Psalm 22:23</u> Lit. *seed*
i. <u>Psalm 22:27</u> *Gentiles*
j. <u>Psalm 22:27</u> So with MT, LXX, Tg.; Arab., Syr., Vg. *Him*
k. <u>Psalm 22:29</u> Death

a. <u>Psalm 23:1</u> *lack*
b. <u>Psalm 23:2</u> Lit. *pastures of tender grass*
c. <u>Psalm 23:2</u> Lit. *waters of rest*
d. <u>Psalm 23:6</u> So with LXX, Syr., Tg., Vg.; MT *return*
e. <u>Psalm 23:6</u> Or *To the end of my days,* lit. *For length of days*

a. <u>Psalm 91:3</u> One who catches birds in a trap or snare

b. <u>Psalm 91:4</u> A small shield
c. <u>Psalm 91:12</u> *lift*
d. <u>Psalm 91:12</u> *strike*
e. <u>Psalm 91:14</u> *exalt him*
f. <u>Psalm 91:16</u> Lit. *length of days*

a. <u>Psalm 103:14</u> Understands our constitution
b. <u>Psalm 103:16</u> *not*
c. <u>Psalm 103:21</u> *servants*

Again, practice...practice...practice singing the word and eating healthy.

Meet the Authors

&

Chefs

Linda D. Lee

Visionary Linda D. Lee is the CEO and Founder of LL Media Group, LLC, a Personal Development Consultancy company. She is a Professional Certified Life Coach (PCLC), Certified Christian Mentor (CCM), International Speaker, Multi award-winning author, 2019 Indie Author Legacy Award Author of the Year (Relationships) and a voice for the voiceless. She has amassed over 20 years' combined experience in personal development, customer service, and emotion management strategies.

Professionally, she is a two-time recipient of: Former President Obama Gold and Bronze Volunteer Service Award, Dallas-Ft. Worth Federal Executive Board Public Service Excellence Recognition Award, and Glynco Law Enforcement Academy. Linda is a graduate of Rockhurst University Business Programmed Course. She is a forerunner of the Human Capital Training Ambassadors Pilot Coaching Program. Currently she is pursuing a dual degree in psychology and leadership.

As a *Family Relationship Midwife,* ® she touches lives through workshops and webinars to build healthy relationships. Linda teaches entrepreneurs how to turn their pain into purposeful tools using sustainability plans, as witnessed in her workshops and speaking engagements in Cape Coast, Ghana, Africa, and London, UK.

To learn more, visit
Facebook & LinkedIn: Linda D. Lee
www.1lindadlee.com

Stephanie Marie Pelle

Stephanie is the founder and creator of the Hope and Healing Facebook page. The purpose of the page is to share cooking and Caribbean inspired recipes using plant-based whole foods. Tutorials are also available to encourage health and wellness.

She retired in 2017 from the Mayo Clinic Arizona after working over 20 years in healthcare, five of which, were in the accounting department. In January 2016, she started Tax Guru, a tax preparation business. She managed the bookkeeping for a successful family owned business, Peltech, LLC, from 2002-2013.

In 2001 she graduated from Scottsdale Community College with an Associate's in Business and continues lifelong learning at Western International University.

To learn more, visit
Facebook: Hope Healing page
HopeHealing01@gmail.com

Vandra Noel

Vandra Noel is a native of Fort Worth, Texas where she wears multiple hats. She is a loving wife, mother, Gigi, daughter and sister. She is an author, entrepreneur, evangelist, hairstylist, caregiver and minister. She studied at the University of North Texas, (UNT), The Bible School of Scripture College, and Ogles Beauty School where she graduated with honors and has been working in the cosmetology field for 27 years. She currently completed the two-year Ministers in Training course at Ambassadors Today Church where she was ordained. Vandra's salon, Shear Ambiance, was awarded Best Salon in 2018 Business Awards.

Vandra has been a caregiver since she was young, giving care to several family members which has increased her knowledge and passion for those battling different illnesses. Her heart's desire is to encourage, empower and edify those who feel like giving up when life happens. Vandra wants her light to shine everyday so that those in darkness can see the Christ within her.

To learn more, visit
Facebook: Vandra Noel
Instagram: Mrs. V. Noel
Astongigi@gmail.com

Latonya Thomas

As the President and CEO of La'She'a Public Relations (LPR), Latonya Thomas known as, "The Preacher's Agent," has dedicated her talents and skills to building LPR into a leading management firm of preeminent distinction.

Founded in January 2010, Latonya Thomas leads all facets of business development for **LPR**. She drives the company to develop key business relationships/partnerships with clients to provide effective business services and add value to their bottom-line.

In June of 2013, a new division of La'She'a public relations was launched. La'She'a Public Relations will focus mainly on providing resources for churches, ministries, artists, authors, record labels, non-profit organizations and small businesses.

Latonya assists, helps, coordinates new, emerging, high-profile entities, non-profit organizations, entrepreneurs, and ministry "thought-leaders" to strategically and effectively leverage new media to reach their goals. Latonya is a native of Orange, Texas.

To learn more visit
Facebook: Latonya Thomas
& Queen "B" Magazine
Instagram: latonyalashea

Chef Nneka

Chef Nneka is the CEO of Dolphin Restaurant and Catering Services in Abuja, Nigeria. She is a Christian, mother and wife.

Nneka is a professional chef and alumni of Red Dish Chronicles Culinary School, Nigeria. She also learned a lot from her mother who has been in the restaurant business for more than four decades. Her legacy still stands today.

In continuing the entrepreneurial legacy, Chef Nneka has been in business cooking the best of Nigerian foods for over 30 years. She has a customer base of over 500 where she serves freshly made Nigerian food and continental cuisines.

Her social proof includes over twenty-two thousand followers on Instagram and three thousand followers on Facebook.

To learn more, visit
E-mail: hi@chefnneka.com
Instagram: @chefnneka
Twitter: @chefnneka
Facebook: @chefnneka

Chef Eboni Dionne

Chef Eboni Dionne is a native of Fort Worth, TX. Her inspiration to pursue the health and wellness field is deeply personal. Her father succumbed to Multiple Sclerosis when she graduated from college. His disease had put a deep question inside of her that she had to find the answer. Why do some people get sick and have their bodies turn against them? How much of that is one's control?

Her professional and educational journey has been very interesting in the accumulation of skills, knowledge and wisdom she has garnered in her 20-year career.

She has earned a B.S. in Biology, Masters of Public Health, Certified Health Coach and is also a Master

Trainer for two Stanford University Evidenced Based classes for Chronic Disease management. She is also a chef that specializes in vegan and vegetarian Soul Food, taking traditional recipes and transforming them into dishes of the most satisfying, delicious meals of balanced sustenance.

She is thrilled to use the culmination of her training and education to improve the lives of the people in her community.

To learn more, visit
Facebook: Chef Eboni Dionne
Instagram: chefebonidionne
www.ChefEboniDionne.com

www.ingramcontent.com/pod-product-compliance
Lightning Source LLC
Chambersburg PA
CBHW071213200326
41519CB00018B/5505